W9-BQM-923

Five Poets
of the Pacific Northwest

FIVE POETS

OF THE PACIFIC NORTHWEST

Kenneth O. Hanson

Richard Hugo

166

Carolyn Kizer

William Stafford

David Wagoner

Edited with an Introduction by
ROBIN SKELTON

Drawings by
CARL MORRIS

University of Washington Press   Seattle and London

Copyright © 1964 by the University of Washington Press
First paperback edition, 1964
First Washington Paperback edition, 1968
Library of Congress Catalog Card Number 64-20489
Printed in the United States of America

*The poems "An Address to the Vacationers at Cape Lookout"
(1950) by William Stafford; "Equestrian in Jalisco" (1954) by
Kenneth O. Hanson; "After Consulting My Yellow Pages"
(1959), "The Fruit of the Tree" (1964), and "The Night of the
Sad Women" (1964) by David Wagoner—copyrighted in the
respective years shown by The New Yorker Magazine, Inc.*

TO THE MEMORY OF

Theodore Roethke

1908-1963

ACKNOWLEDGMENTS

KENNETH O. HANSON. Nine of these poems have appeared in *Poetry Northwest*: "In Springtime," "Goodbye for Being Right," "Spring," "The Divide," "Montana," "Snow," "Before the Storm," "The Distance Anywhere," and "Making the Scene." Two others—"San Miguel de Allende, Gto." and "Elegiac"—first appeared in *Sewanee Review*. The author retains sole copyright for "Protocol," "On Releasing a Captive Wild Goose," "One at the E Moon," "Getting a Shine on the Ginza," "A Going Concern," and "One Night."

RICHARD HUGO. "Ocean on Monday," "Neighbor," "Digging Is an Art," and "The Way a Ghost Dissolves" appeared in *A Run of Jacks* (University of Minnesota Press, 1962). The other poems, for which the author retains copyright, will be included in *Death of the Kapowsin Tavern*, to be published by Harcourt, Brace, and World, Inc. in 1965; the individual poems have previously been published as follows: "The Other Grave," *Choice*; "In Stafford Country," *Poetry*; "The Blonde Road," *Carleton Miscellany*; "Death of the Kapowsin Tavern," *Kenyon Review*; "Duwamish Head," *Poetry Northwest*.

CAROLYN KIZER. Four of these poems—"The Great Blue Heron," "By the Riverside," "A Widow in Wintertime," and "Tying One on in Vienna"—appeared in *The Ungrateful Garden* (Indiana University Press, 1961). "Amusing Our Daughters" appeared in *Choice*; "Summer Near the River" in *The Partisan Review*; "Pro Femina" in *Carleton Miscellany*. Others have appeared in *The Spectator*. The author retains the copyright for "Winter Song."

WILLIAM STAFFORD. The poems included here have been published as follows: "Walking West," "Watching the Jet Planes Dive," "Lore," "Outside," and "At the Bomb Testing Site" in *West of Your City* (The Talisman Press, 1960); "In the Night Desert," "Found in a Storm," "Traveling Through the Dark," "In the Museum," "A Dedication," "Late at Night," and "Fall Wind" in *Traveling Through the Dark* (Harper and Row, 1962); "Bulletin" in *Experiment*; "Believing What I Know" in *Saturday Review*; "To a Colleague Fulbrighting in Finland" in *Voices*; "Ultimate Problems" in *Poetry Northwest*; "On an Island in the San Juans" in *Poetry*; "Peace Walk" in *Focus/Midwest*; "Letter from Oregon" in *Western Humanities Review*.

DAVID WAGONER. The five poems from *The Nesting Ground* (Indiana University Press, 1963) are "After Consulting My Yellow Pages," "Diary," "Elegy for Simon Corl, Botanist," "Out for a Night," and "A Guide to Dungeness Spit." Of these, "Elegy for Simon Corl, Botanist" has appeared in *Saturday Review*; "Out for a Night" in *The Massachusetts Review*; "A Guide to Dungeness Spit" in *Hudson Review*. "Murder Mystery," from *A Place to Stand* (Indiana University Press, 1958), also appeared in *Poetry*, as did "Leaving Something Behind." The author retains the copyright for "Observations from the Outer Edge," "After Falling," "The Poets Agree to be Quiet by the Swamp," and "The Man of the House."

CONTENTS

Carolyn Kizer

William Stafford

David Wagoner

INTRODUCTION

GOOD POETS rarely fit easily into "schools," and the five poets presented here are no exception. Each has an individual voice and vision. Nevertheless, there is reason in grouping them together, for they are all, by birth or by long custom, natives of the Pacific Northwest, and, in different ways, have taken much from their environment.

Those aspects of his environment which most affect a poet are not necessarily geographical, of course. They may be linguistic and sociological as well as geological and botanical. In the case of the Pacific Northwest, the dominant feature of the poetic environment for a number of years was the presence of Theodore Roethke, and, as a teacher and visionary, he affected the poets of the area in more, and in less superficial, ways than any "influence-hunter" could detect. More than one poet has found Roethke's courage and devotion to his vocation an inspiriting example, and has been urged forward to further experiments and explorations. As a teacher, Roethke, like many major poets, emphasized the importance of attention to detail; he made clear the basic significance of syntax, punctuation, and controlled prosody, and gave his pupils and his friends fresh insights into the fundamentals of the poetic craft. Some may think this an unimportant contribution to human knowledge, but all poets will agree that there is no more valuable critic than the one who puts his finger upon the previously unnoticed weakness of a verse, and who is capable of explaining and insisting upon the value of a precise craftsmanship. It is this critic, and this teacher, who most surely leads each individual toward the discovery and exploitation of his unique voice. Roethke, both as a university teacher and as a writer, taught in this way. The many different voices of the Northwest are, in part, a tribute to his influence, and it is proper that this collection of five of them should be dedicated to his memory.

Although I have said that there are many different voices in the Northwest, I must also say that the poets have all been deeply affected by their physical environment. It is obvious that, in this area, the landscape must have a powerful influence upon the art created within it. Some poets have gone directly to the sea, the rivers, the forests, and the mountains for their imagery; others have avoided direct description; all, however, appear to have had the sense of place imprinted firmly upon their sensibilities. The poetry written in deserts and in cities, though it may refer to specific places, and even depend upon sympathy with some particular spot, rarely makes full use of natural imagery. That is to say, the perpetual interpenetration of the savage and the domestic, and the continual awareness of solitude, mortality, and history do not present themselves inevitably in terms of landscape. In much of the poetry of the Northwest these themes do appear, and frequently they are connected to the Washington, Oregon, and British Columbian shores, mountains, and forests.

This may suggest that, in the Northwest, there is a good deal of "regionalism." Certainly some poets (like Richard Hugo) do find it helpful to work in terms of a definable region. Others, however (like Carolyn Kizer and Kenneth Hanson), range far afield. The Northwest is a more recently settled area than the Northeast; here, still, the vast majority of people are aware of a cultural inheritance which is not primarily American. Moreover, the very wildness of much of the landscape, and the presence of some of the most artistically rich Indian tribes on the continent, make people aware of the relationship between old cultures and new, primitive ways of life and sophisticated ones. Thus many poets in this area find themselves drawn to the sympathetic exploration of ancient cultures, and especially those of the

Orient, which seem almost nearer than those of Europe. Chinese and Japanese culture is an important aspect of the Northwest scene. We get poets working simultaneously in the context of one of the youngest and one of the most ancient settled societies in the world.

It would be silly to be too dogmatic over such imponderables, but, looking at the poetry written on this coast, it does appear that the awareness of a mixed cultural inheritance is an important part of each poet's sensibility. The departure of a poet for Italy (where Richard Hugo has just gone), or for Greece (whence Kenneth Hanson has just returned), is, in this situation, much less an escape from the Northwest environment than a further exploration of it. This has, of course, been said before, and about Americans and Canadians from all parts of the continent, and it has been true. It is still, and intensely, true now in the Northwest.

Of the poets here, Kenneth Hanson appears to range the farthest afield for his subject matter. His poems refer to Mexico, Greece, Japan, and Italy, as well as to many areas of North America. There is a difference between a poem's ostensible subject matter and its theme, however, and though Hanson's subject matter is various, his theme is less so. The majority of his poems present the lyric moment at the center of the enormous hurrying world. This moment is reached by way of a precisely cadenced language that depends for its effect as much upon its silences as its statements. Thus, in "Making the Scene" the speaker does not defend himself against the accusation that his poems fail to deal with the "larger issues," but presents the image of a scholar

> stopped by to copy

> a song from a notebook—
> anxious to get
> the set of the words just right.

This precision of mind *is*, it is implied, one of the largest of issues. Those who attempt to solve the world's problems by explicit analysis so often end by falsifying the situation. We must recognize that

> Sometimes
> a thing can be made
> too clear.

It is often in the smallest incidents that the human situation can most easily be seen. The whole storm of mortal conflict is made immediately vivid to us by the contemplation of the dead whale's jelly eye, and the authority of the natural world comes home to us when we discuss the different ways in which poets and geographers speak of rivers, mountains, and islands.

These are poems devoted to the contemplative individual, distrustful of generalizations and of easy answers. The pursuit of happiness is less important than the sense of personal identity.

> But hell what the hell
> I say I don't
> have to be happy I
> just have to be alive.

In all these poems the self-assured poise of certain people and certain objects is presented for our admiration. The lady from Fu-kien may break all the city ordinances, but her "fabulous speech" with its "syllables of that exacter scale" makes the whole world clear to us, and the room described in "Interior" is so completely itself as to possess the beauty of inevitable form. The bamboo, too, in being true to its nature, presents us with a fact that may disturb our usual notions, but which carries all the authority of the incontrovertible.

> to bend
> is not necessarily
> to give in

Thus, behind all Hanson's poems is an almost oriental passion for the precisely poised image, which, in its clarity, indicates a decorum and an integrity that should be a part of all human conduct. The language of the poems is at one with their import; the structure is also the message, and the message is a tone of voice as well as a formulation.

In all good poetry the structure and the meaning are inseparable, of course. Richard Hugo's language is as completely a part of his theme as is Hanson's. His world is, however, a violent one, and his poems are often built up by means of apparently crude lists of images, block upon block, as if he were building a dry-stone wall. Thus in "Duwamish Head" we get:

> My vision started at this river mouth,
> On a slack tide, trying to catch bullheads
> In a hopeless mud. The pier was caving
> From the weight of gulls. Wail of tug
> And trawl, a town not growing up
> Across the bay. . . .

Such lines have a factual drive and a nervous energy that are wholly convincing. The speaker of these poems is wrestling with the brute realities of his world; each perception is another lunge or twist and demands another effort of will and muscle. Indeed, much of Hugo's poetry is an attempt to portray man as a creature attempting to keep its balance in the teeth of a storm which is both physical and metaphysical. The spiritual wasteland of the shore upon a gray Monday morning, where "gray coordinates with nothing" is not presented passively. Though the solitude of the individual is clearly implied by the jelly-fish "that open lonely as a hand," the space

> . . . drives into expanse,
> boredom banging in your face,
> the horizon stiff with strain.

There is no rest, no ease, no comfortable self-pity here; man must fight his environment.

This battle is a hectic one, and the enemy is, finally, unconquerable.

> I planned to cheat the road with laughter.
> Build a home no storm could crack
> And sing my Fridays over centuries of water—
> Once more, have me back, my awkward weather—
> But the land is not for sale. Centuries
> Are strung: a blonde road north and south
> And no man will improve it with macadam.

This stanza from "The Blonde Road" shows how Hugo has made his landscape reflect the predicament of the man of our time who has survived one war only to discover another. It was silly of us to imagine that the world would settle down; our days continue to be disturbed both by memories and by the violence inherent in the forces of nature.

Hugo's poetry is tough, violent, tragic. His world is largely a ruined one, but it contains men who have the courage to face that ruin, and, as a consequence, even the most bitter poems are positive rather than negative, and their energy is triumphant.

> If I say love
> Was here, along the river, show me bones
> Of cod, scales and blood, faces in the clouds
> So thick they jam the sky with laughter.

The laughter here is the laughter of the makar who can stare down the gaze of the Fates.

Laughter also plays a part in Carolyn Kizer's work, for she is an ironist of great cunning, as well as a lyricist. Indeed, of the five poets in this book she is easily the most versatile. In "Pro Femina" she uses a naturally cadenced hexameter that moves easily from the colloquial to the rhetorical and back again without losing its identity. In "Tying One on in Vienna" the form is freer; the lines are of different lengths, and the tone varies from the exuberant to the sardonic and the sentimental. In both these poems the language is direct, witty, and forceful. Indeed, "Pro Femina" is a great deal more Juvenalian than any translation of Juvenal that I have yet read.

Astringent wit and irony form only one facet of Miss Kizer's work, however. In other poems it is her delicacy and particularity which are exciting. Take the opening of "The Great Blue Heron" as an example.

> As I wandered on the beach
> I saw the heron standing
> Sunk in the tattered wings
> He wore as a hunchback's coat.
> Shadow without a shadow,
> Hung on invisible wires
> From the top of a canvas day,
> What scissors cut him out?
> Superimposed on a poster
> Of summer by the strand
> Of a long-decayed resort,
> Poised in the dusty light
> Some fifteen summers ago;
> I wondered, an empty child,
> "Heron, whose ghost are you?"

The image of the heron is presented with great precision and visual clarity, and all the physical details of its appearance are related to the themes of memory, weariness, and grief, which the poem is about to explore. The economy and reticence of this poem are characteristic of much of Miss Kizer's nonsatirical work; they are central to her versions of Chinese poems, and they give many of her other lyrics their individual strength. In many poems they combine with the natural cadences and easy colloquialism of real artistic authority to give us work of astonishing subtlety and strength.

> I am as monogamous as the North Star
> But I don't want you to know it. You'd only take advantage.

> While you are fickle as spring sunlight.
> All right, sleep! The cat means more to you than I.
> I can rouse you, but then you swagger out.
> I glimpse you from the window, striding towards the river.

This stanza of "Summer Near the River" not only makes use of a Shakespearean echo in its first line, but also uses the most colloquial of expressions, and fuses both tones of voice into a rhythmically assured and balanced whole.

It is not possible to sum up the world of Miss Kizer's poetry as easily as those of Kenneth Hanson or Richard Hugo, for it is more various. If there is one attitude which emerges more frequently than any other, however, it is one of affection. Tender, or passionate, or rollicking, or satiric, these poems seem always to include an affection for people and a detestation of hypocrisy and inhumanity.

William Stafford's poems are also difficult to sum up in this way, for his themes are also numerous. Nevertheless, it is obvious that his foremost characteristic is a deceptive directness and simplicity. Perhaps the most striking instance of this is "Fall Wind," whose very title is ambiguous, hinting at mortality and the fall of man, as well as referring to autumn. Ambiguity is central to Stafford's work, but it is not the riddling ambiguity of the academic wit; it is rather the plurivalence of the symbolist. Thus in "At the Bomb Testing Site," the lizard waits for a "change" which remains undefined and therefore the more disturbing. This poem is also a good example of Stafford's particular kind of "commitment." Although he never presents an explicitly political attitude, his poems often include political and sociological observations. "Watching the Jet Planes Dive" is not a pacifist poem, but it is a poem about man's predicament in a war-threatened and bellicose age, and it discovers in the particular and ephemeral a universal and timeless condition.

> We must find something forgotten by everyone alive,
> and make some fabulous gesture when the sun goes down

> as they do by custom in little Mexico towns
> where they crawl for some ritual up a rocky steep.
> The jet planes dive; we must travel on our knees.

Stafford's poetry almost always moves from an apparently direct presentation of the concrete and particular toward a sense of the almost numinous unknown.

> At that corner in a flash of lightning we two stood;
> that glimpse we had will stare through the dark forever:
> on the poorest roads we would be walkers and beggars,
> toward some deathless meeting involving a crust of bread.

This movement toward mystery often results in an enigmatic poetry which each reader must interpret in his own way. Thus "Believing What I Know" ends with a stanza of gnomic simplicity and mystery.

> I learn from the land. Some day
> like a field I may take the next thing
> so well that whatever is will be me.

The bare, direct diction of William Stafford is in sharp contrast to the crowded and vigorous language of David Wagoner, whose poetry is filled with metaphysical conceits, burlesque humor, and intense symbolism. His exuberance and wit are well displayed in "After Consulting My Yellow Pages":

> All went well today in the barbers' college:
> The razor handles pointed gracefully outward,
> The clippers were singing like locusts. And far away
> On the fox farms, the red and silver sun brushed lightly
> Tail after tail. Happily, the surveyors
> Measured the downhill pasture through a theodolite,
> Untroubled by birchtrees. . . .

Wagoner's gaiety is never merely entertaining, however; he develops his exuberant fancies toward a metaphysical interpretation of the world around him. Moreover, the world he interprets is shrewdly observed as well as cleverly transformed. In such poems as "Elegy for Simon Corl, Botanist" and "The Poets Agree to be Quiet by the Swamp," he reveals a visual sharpness worthy of Marvell. The former poem is Marvell-like also in the cool balance of its diction and in the deft organization of pastoral symbolism. Wagoner, in fact, is more truly a "metaphysical" and "wit" than any other poet in this anthology. His imagery is often bizarre, but always dexterously handled and intellectually satisfactory. Moreover, he has managed to avoid that tiresome allusiveness and sententious pedantry which so often appears in the work of twentieth-century followers of the Metaphysical Tradition. Thus, while the total approach of such poems as "The Man of the House" may remind us of the work of several of his contemporaries, the imagery and diction are completely his own, vital, and decisive.

> In safety shoes going down basement stairs,
> He'd flick his rewired rearrangement of lights
> And chase all shadows into the coalbin
> Where they could watch him, blinking at his glare.
> If shadows hadn't worked, he would have made them.

This in its ease of tone, concreteness of imagery, and beautifully controlled symbolism, is typical of Wagoner's work. He is working within, and developing, a tradition which, in the work of his contemporaries, has too often resulted in mere cleverness. The extent to which he has enriched and enlivened the tradition can easily be seen in the enormous vigor of "Diary," and in the outrageous burlesque of "Murder Mystery," which moves from farcical parody to real pathos without any difficulty at all. Like all the poets presented here, Wagoner is a masterly technician and has a completely individual voice.

That is, perhaps, the most significant thing about the poets in this book, and about the poets of the Northwest in general. Living, as they do, in an area of immense natural and cultural variety, their poetry has not conformed to any one pattern. Though it is possible to trace certain aspects of their environment as important influences upon their poetry, and in particular to note the oriental element and the effect of landscape, it is not possible to pretend, even for a second, that they form a "school." These are simply five of the good poets now working in this area. Were it not that it was decided to give a good deal of space to a few poets rather than to give a few pages each to many, the number of poets here could have been doubled, trebled, or even quadrupled. I myself deeply regret the absence of several poets from these pages, but I could not wish any of these five to be omitted, any more than I could wish any of them to have less space. This book, therefore, is only a sample of the work being written in the Pacific Northwest, but it is, I believe, an exciting one, and I, as a recent arrival in the area, am proud to have been given the opportunity to make it.

ROBIN SKELTON

The University of Victoria, B.C.

Five Poets
of the Pacific Northwest

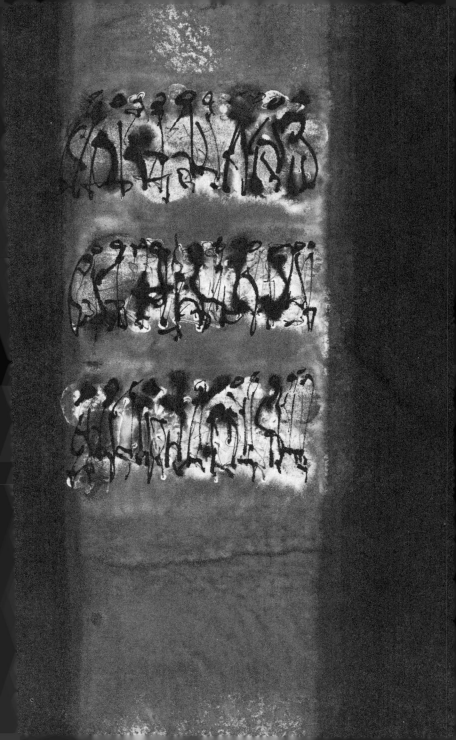

Kenneth O. Hanson was born in Shelley,
Idaho, in 1922. He was educated at the University
of Idaho and the University of Washington. A
folio of 8 Poems was privately printed in a very
limited edition in 1958, and a first collection is
now in preparation. He is at present Professor of
Literature and Humanities at Reed College.

In Springtime

after Lin Ho-ching

Surrounded by
anything growing
I stop and think.

The crane stands
on one leg among
lilies. The bees go

bumbling in and out
of the flowers.
Wine slows me down.

I poke and prod
at the roots of things
and remember

too late how fond
the painters were
of stairs that lead nowhere.

Goodbye for Being Right

Having read once in
The National Geographic
"Who for the Soochow Ho"
(*ho* being river)
and having admired
that resonance

—having observed
during World War II
spun flat across Texas
a country hit tune
called "Iwo Jima's Isle"
(*jima* being isle)

—and having further
heard the Fox (being old Ez)
in a remarkable cadence
tell us who "with
herds and with cohorts
looked on Mt. Taishan"
(*shan* being mountain)

I bring these instances
together, more to instruct
than to delight, more
to delight than in despair
knowing that everywhere

war or no war
the geographers are always
right, and the poets
when they try to put space

around words are brought
to a blankness

—the floating island
holds in the distance as
the imperial mountain holds
and the wide world opens
arid and bright and clear
faced with a silence.

San Miguel de Allende, Gto.

Again this morning, American painters
are painting the church in the plaza.
The teacher is saying, "To catch the light
's the trick. Dutch light is domestic,
French is a plant that grows too green.
This light lacks all direction, falls
like a bundle of sticks, or is southern,
watery, and flows." They peer at the church
through the watery southern light
while the morning goes on around them.

Cicadas are giving an edge to the air
as Ezequiel Torres, *chine* boy, greets *"El avión!"*
the drunk at 11 a.m., weaving beautifully,
like a butterfly, toward the cage of the Cucaracha,
and mustachioed police with squirt guns
are annihilating fleas in the six local taxis.

O what will the ladies from Punxsatawney,
Twin Lakes, or Drain, Oregon, keep
of this morning so filled with implacable
foreign birds? Will they remember the slicker
hawking his magical root cure-all
in the market, the rain saint chanted
with crosses and thorns uphill to Querétaro
and every day opening with burros and bells?

Perhaps. But always when the northern season
turns anfractuous and spare, against the bells
and the flies and the kite in the distance
they will hear the voice of the instructor

praising the canvas that came between them and the scene
and bore the innocent truths of art, the church
in a wobbly line, and Ezequiel in spite of himself
home through customs, into a light solid as stone.

Twice for a Small Song

1. Spring

The black cat has folded
himself on his knees
under the apple tree.

Blossoms are falling.
One has fallen on his nose.
He is a tiger in Mozambique.

He ignores the postman
passing. Come, cat
quiet as a kumquat. There

are no tigers in Mozambique.
The postman is passing.
Blossoms are falling.

2. Protocol

: or to say with the cat
(bright Apollo
brought down
to his tin pan)
"I prefer an
elegant simplicity"

Say, "This night
breeds crickets"

or "Walls (waltz)
a glisten of bottles
in stone"

Sometimes
a thing can be made
too clear.

The Divide

after Lin Ho-ching

I confess I get moony
when I see these
out of the way places.

Parked for a minute
I look down at
the clapboard houses.

Foot of the hill
I drink spring water
so cold my back teeth ache.

God! childhood!
how soon I forgot it!

Montana

after Lin Ho-ching

Just over the border
a handful of stores
both sides of the road—
grocery, filling station, feed store
drug store, depot, tavern.

I wait on the platform
for the one daily train south.
The vapors of summer rise over the rails
and the dust shines, north and south.
From somewhere a black dog
is going home obliquely.

After three months
I still don't much want to leave.
Every day like today—acrid & flat & spare
but with beautiful small signs
as August dies.

Now there's a fat blues
spilling from the door of Ed's Happy Haven
and the neon comes on
(before night does)
seeming to say to me Don't
go   Don't go   Come back

Snow

after Lin Ho-ching

Eight
a.m. with the doors
and windows drifted shut—
how could there be
any dust on the knobby sculpture?

The day
is as self-contained
as the life of a stylite—
pure as "Persimmons"
by Mu-ch'i.

Step
out and the sidewalks crack.
Brisk willows
don't budge in the snow.

Stone
sober this morning
I can't bear the thought
of deliberate action—not

with the world
so shined by the weather.

Before the Storm

One summer, high in Wyoming
we drove nine miles and paid
to see the great whale, pickled
and hauled on a flatcar crosscountry.
"Throat no bigger'n a orange,"
the man said, in a smell to high
heaven. I wondered how Jonah
could weather that rubbery household
tangled in fish six fathoms down.
Now, beached by the sun and
shunted to a siding, the gray
beast lay dissolving in chains.

It was none of my business
late in the day, while overhead
Stars and Stripes Forever played
in a national breeze, to sidle
past ropes and poke with a ginger
finger, nostril and lip and eye
till Hey! said the man, keep away
from my whale! But too late,
too late. I had made my mark.
The eye in its liquid socket swung,
the jaw clanged shut, and all the way home
through the bone-dry gullies I could
hear the heart as big as a bushel
beat. O weeks I went drowned
while red-winged grasshoppers span
like flying fish, and the mile-high
weather gathered its forces.

Elegiac

Morning, this morning wakes me
to April, nostalgia, insouciant
season, whose importance
like the ambition of the Romans
is chiefly historical. I
remember Quinn's, where fat Sylvia
tended bar, bleached blond;

the beer was rich, the glasses full
and Spring came staggering up the hill
to light with his riot forsythia,
the flowering plum on 42nd,
and expire in a thirst at the door.
Loggers, householders, a renegade
scholar: *numero deus impare gaudet:*

what a bunch of characters, Quinn
said, very Roman, who one day tired
of dice, music, good fellowship
and gave his name to a fishmarket
in the north end of town, a change
the world widely ignored. O
this morning I think of it sadly.

The Distance Anywhere

My neighbor, a lady from Fu-kien
has rearranged her yard completely.
She has cut down the willow tree,
burning it, piecemeal, against a city
ordinance, and has put in its place
her garden of strange herbs.

I confess I resent the diligence
her side of the fence—the stink
of that oriental spinach she hangs
on the clothesline to dry, and the squawk
of the chicken I suspect she keeps,
against a city ordinance, shut up
in the white garage, eventual soup.

But when, across the rows of what-
ever she grows, she brings her
fabulous speech to bear, birds
in the trees, the very butterflies
unbend, acknowledging, to syllables
of that exacter scale, she'd make
the neighborhood, the unaccustomed
air, for all the world to see,
sight, sound and smell, Fu-kien,
beyond our ordinances, clear.

Equestrian in Jalisco

Dark eyed, the children stare
from doorways of white houses
where shopworn pigeons are
cooing on all the roofs.

Staring, they watch the soldier
ride into the burnished square,
ride up to the pink cathedral
frosted with flowery saints
like a great rococo cake
and dismount with a jingle.

In another minute he will speak
and they will vanish forever
mysterious as flights of birds
And in the cavernous silence
the polished dust will drift

where the soldier, mounted again
on his black horse, holds a classic pose
forever in the empty square
and bound in hoops of iron
slowly his cold eyes burn.

On Releasing a Captive Wild Goose

after Po Chu-i

Chiang-chou, my first winter there, snow fell thick.
The Yangtze froze over and trees broke under the fallen
   snow.
Starving, small birds flew this way and that
and with them a wild goose, honking in hunger.
It pecked at the crusted snowbank, sat hunched on the
   frozen river,
tried to fly, wobbled, and river boys caught it with nets.
They brought it to market alive, where I bought it—
an exile here myself, a northerner in the south
who moved by another exile, ransomed and set you free
and you take to the clouds.

Wild goose, grey exile, where will you head for?
Not north for Huai-hsi, where ten thousand rebels are still
   undefeated!
An army on one side, one on the other grow old in the
   facing camps
their rations so short they'd welcome even someone like you.
Starved soldiers, they'd shoot you down, pick your bones
use your long feathers to give wings to their arrows!

Interior

These things are round: the wheel
where this woman seems to spin,
staring at fields outside the window,
the rug where a cat is curled in
the geometric center, these few
copper pots and a dark platter.
Everything else is strict with corners.
The light where it enters the window
is flat, the color of butter, and the sea
if there is a sea beyond the fields
is perfectly flat. From the picture
it is difficult to imagine that the wheel
has ever turned, or that the woman
looking beyond the fields could ever
guess the rummage of the sea, or that
this light could shine too on the fierce
intricate tropics, or the sun like butter
could burn itself down to a cinder
or ever be anything but round.

One at the & Moon

Six weeks and two typhoons away,
beached in a foreign bar
whose name has no meaning,
molding like Sidney Greenstreet from
some rash or a tropical fungus,
I try to concentrate on
the text for today.
"The sage delights in water,
the poet takes to the hills."

Outside this air-conditioned time
a garden repeats the scroll
and I watch the elegant waterfall
fall past what seem to be
the mountains of Kweilin.
There are blank spaces on the wall.

On the wall, the lizard moves
with the rhythm of an early movie.
Twin joys. *Shuang Hsi.*
The plum wine blossoms in the blood
and I hear somewhere under
the rocks and the water the sound
of a world slowly turning. What
is empty? What is full? Only the four
corners of the past stand pat.

Getting a Shine on the Ginza

Remembering later
how they bow
how the waiter
stood
how the conductor
took off his cap
I think
there is room
for a garden
anywhere—

"The bean curd
bakes over char
coal flaming like
lotus blossoms"

or take the bamboo—
to bend
is not necessarily
to give in

A Going Concern

Speeding on hair-
raising hairpin turns
through the Peloponnese
having missed
Mycenae for Messene

taking one hand
from the wheel
to cross himself
at every Dangerous Curve
my pious pimp friend
tells me Hanson be
happy. Do me the favor.

But hell what the hell
I say I don't
have to be happy I
just have to be alive.

One Night

with Manuel Izquierdo
talking to Tomasito
the scab, the strikebreaker
though I only
found this out later

I first saw him as
the dark lady killer
white teeth, thin mustache
who kept saying Man
I don't dig your sculpture
and buying the beer

which made me wonder
till I found out he'd
married a fast blond
with 2 kids—a big house
a big car—and what
can you do most places

a Mexican

Making the Scene

after Lin Ho-ching

One notable critic complains
my poems don't deal
with the larger issues.

I look at Mt. Pilchuck
in spring, under a green rain
dripping from the eaves.

Well, there are some
would put the gull down
for not wanting to be an eagle

and the lizard
for changing quick as a wink.
From where I sit

new pine-shoots glisten
over Queen Anne's lace
at the foot of the meadow

and one day last week
a guitar-playing scholar
stopped by to copy

a song from a notebook—
anxious to get
the set of the words just right.

Richard Hugo was born in Seattle, Washington, in 1923. He was educated at the University of Washington. His first collection of poems, A Run of Jacks, *appeared in 1962, and a second book,* Death of the Kapowsin Tavern, *will be published early in 1965. At present he teaches English at Montana State University in Missoula.*

In Stafford Country

No hills. Raw wind unchecked, brings word
Of death from Texas. No shade. Sun bruises
The oats gold. With homes exposed
No wonder people love. Farms absorb
The quiet of the snow, and birds
Are black and nameless miles away.

Without a shield of hills, a barricade
Of elms, one resorts to magic, hiding
The joker well behind the gesturing hand.
Childish wars continue in our minds.
Paint is the gray it was in Carthage.

Where land is flat, words are far apart.
Each word is seen, coming from far off,
A calm storm, almost familiar, across
The plain. The word floats by, alive.
Homes are empty and the love goes on
As the odor of grain jumps in the wind.

Tahola

Where sea breaks inland, claiming the Quinalt
In a half saltwater lake, canoes turn gray
Waiting for the runs. The store makes money
But the two cafes, not open, rot in spray.
Baskets you can buy are rumored Cherokee.
When kings run wild, girls use salmon oil
To stain a doll's face real. The best house
Was never envied for its tile. Cars
And philosophic eyes are coated by the sea.

Whites pay well to motor up the river,
Harvest blackmouth, humpbacks, silvers,
Jacks and sea run cuts. Where rain assaults
The virgin timber and the fishpools boil,
The whites pry stories from the guide
With bourbon. Sunset, and they putt downriver
Singing. But the wind, the sea
Make all music language, dead as a wet drum.

When whites drive off and the money's gone
A hundred mongrels bark. Indians
Should mend the tribal nets in moonlight,
Not drink more and hum a white man's tune
They heard upstream. What about the words?
Something about war, translated by the sea
And wind into a song a doll sang
Long ago, riding a crude wave in.

Ocean on Monday

Here at last is ending.
Where gray coordinates with nothing
the horizon wrinkles in the wind.

These will end: shrimp a mile
below, blue shark, sole,
rocks alive as crabs in shifting green,

patent bathers, barnacles, kelp that lies
in wilting whips, jelly-
fish that open lonely as a hand,

space that drives into expanse,
boredom banging in your face,
the horizon stiff with strain.

Neighbor

The drunk who lives across the street from us
fell in our garden, on the beet patch
yesterday. So polite. Pardon me,
he said. He had to be helped up and held,
steered home and put to bed, declaring
we got to have another drink and smile.

I admit my envy. I've found him in salal
and flat on his face in lettuce, and bent
and snoring by that thick stump full of rain
we used to sail destroyers on.
And I've carried him home so often
stone to the rain and me, and cheerful.

I try to guess what's in that dim warm mind.
Does he think about horizoned firs
black against the light, thirty years
ago, and the good girl — what's her name —
believing, or think about the dog
he beat to death that day in Carbonado?

I hear he's dead, and wait now on my porch.
He must be in his shack. The wagon's
due to come and take him where they take
late alcoholics, probably called Farm's End.
I plan my frown, certain he'll be carried out
bleeding from the corners of his grin.

Digging Is an Art

Now they bury her and the clouds run scared.
Elms and the cemetery hedges whine.
Sky shakes in the Bible and the coffin swings.
Now dirt raps on the coffin until wind
and the indifferent cars rip away the choir
from our eyes. Pour the dirt on, digger.
Shovel faster. Sink her where she lies.

For she was harsh as dirt. Her voice crawled
down the garden like a weed, and yet
potatoes bloomed, the beets and carrots
shoved their greens beyond her hymn.
The rock of ages crumbled into soil.
Then the corn came, swaying like her dream
of daddy hanging from a harness in the barn.

At nine on Sunday, those magnetic chimes
five blocks away, her only decent dress,
her rapid stride as if the world would burn,
her envy of the latest cars that passed—
her husband was a failure and the bells
made up for all the luxury she missed.
But he had been defeated by her voice.

Bang the Bible hard in broken rhythm.
She fertilizes soil despite her coffin.
That grass is lucky growing near her stone,
the marker of an enemy of growth.
Shovel, digger. Seal the day forever.
Wet the dirt. The weight will shut her mouth.
A midget spade is digging for a man.

Before I run forever down that dark long wind,
killed by bells, my head split open
by ingratiating clangs, I'll worm my way
into that ground no digger recommends.
Plant the headstone anywhere between champagnes
and drink until you sweat. The wind will bring
you money and the choir keep you clean.

The Way a Ghost Dissolves

Where she lived the close remained the best.
The nearest music and the static cloud,
sun and dirt were all she understood.
She planted corn and left the rest
to elements, convinced that God
with giant faucets regulates the rain
and saves the crops from frost or foreign wind.

Fate assisted her with special cures.
Rub a half potato on your wart
and wrap it in a damp cloth. Close
your eyes and whirl three times and throw.
Then bury rag and spud exactly where
they fall. The only warts that I have now
are memories or comic on my nose.

Up at dawn. The earth provided food
if worked and watered, planted green
with rye grass every fall. Or driven wild
by snakes that kept the carrots clean,
she butchered snakes and carrots with a hoe.
Her screams were sea birds in the wind,
her chopping—nothing like it now.

I will garden on the double run,
my rhythm obvious in ringing rakes,
and trust in fate to keep me poor and kind
and work until my heart is short,
then go out slowly with a feeble grin,
my fingers flexing but my eyes gone gray
from cramps and the lack of oxygen.

Forget the tone. Call the neighbor's trumpet
golden as it grates. Exalt the weeds.
Say the local animals have class
or help me say that ghost has gone to seed.
And why attempt to see the cloud again—
the screaming face it was before it cracked
in wind from Asia and a wanton rain.

The Blonde Road

This road dips and climbs but never bends.
The line it finally is, strings far beyond
My sight, still the color of useless dirt.
Trees are a hundred greens in varying light
As sky breaks black on silver over and in
The sea. Not one home or car. No shacks
Abandoned to the storms. On one side,
Miles of high grass; on the other, weather
And the sea reflecting tons of a wild day.

The wind is from Malay. Tigers in the wind
Make lovers claw each other orange. Blonde
Dirt rises to recite the lies of summer
Before the wind goes north and cats rip
White holes in the sky. Fields are grim
And the birds along this road are always stone.

I planned to cheat the road with laughter.
Build a home no storm could crack
And sing my Fridays over centuries of water—
Once more, have me back, my awkward weather—
But the land is not for sale. Centuries
Are strung: a blonde road north and south
And no man will improve it with macadam.

The road is greased by wind. Sun has turned
The blonde dirt brown, the brown grass
Black and dark ideas of the ocean
Silver. Each month rolls along the road
With an hour's effort. Now the lovers
Can't recall each other or identify
That roar: the northern pain of tigers.

I know that just a word I'll never have
Could make the brown road blonde again
And send the stone birds climbing to their names.

Death of the Kapowsin Tavern

I can't ridge it back again from char.
Not one board left. Only ash a cat explores
And shattered glass smoked black and strung
About from the explosion I believe
In the reports. The white school up for sale
For years, most homes abandoned to the rocks
Of passing boys—the fire, helped by wind
That blew the neon out six years before,
Simply ended lots of ending.

A damn' shame. Now, when the night chill
Of the lake gets in a troller's bones
Where can the troller go for bad wine
Washed down frantically with beer?
And when wise men are in style again
Will one recount the two mile glide of cranes
From dead pines or the nameless yellow
Flowers thriving in the useless logs,
Or dots of light all night about the far end
Of the lake, the dawn arrival of the idiot
With catfish—most of all, above the lake
The temple and our sanctuary there?

Nothing dies as slowly as a scene.
The dusty juke box cracking through
The cackle of a beered up crone—
Wagered wine—sudden need to dance—
These remain in the black debris.
Although, I know in time the lake will send
Wind black enough to blow it all away.

Hideout

In the reeds, the search for food by grebes
Is brief. Each day, inside the shack
The wind paints white, a man keeps warm
By listening to ships go by, keeps sane
By counting european faces
Passing north in clouds. Tugs deposit
Miles of logs outside. A tax collector
Couldn't find this place with holy maps.

When salmon crowd each other
In the river, and the river boils
With recreation's anger, what tall man
Recreates too clearly domes of mills
Downstream, and the gradual opening
As if the river loved the city
Or was crying loudly "take me" to the sea.
What odd games children play.
One shouts himself into a president.
Another pins the villain salmon
To the air with spears. A rowboat
Knocks all night against a pile.

Morning brings a new wind and a new
White coat of weather for the shack.
The salmon moved upstream last night
And no bird cuts the river, looking
For a smelt. Ships sail off to Naples
And the bent face bobbing in the wake
Was counted in another cloud gone north.

The Other Grave

Long and smelling good, the cemetery grass
Could be a kiss. You failed a field
Of Ypsilanti wheat. Below your stone
You never try to touch her there beside you.
I used to blame your failure on the moon.

When old, you needed words like "lake."
"Lake" I'd say. Your eyes began to farm.
Horses took you and a friend where coves
Were wonderful with bass—bluegills
Clowning for your rind below the log.
Catfish ran five pounds. See my picture.
See my mustache then. Any photo fades.
You remain in yellow with your catch.

I'd like to sing you, point each word
About you up and shoot. Wasn't gold
Too easy for your maps, or love
Too simple for your brilliant arms?
I said a British wind was in your face—
Only blue the undertaker planned.
The tunes you hummed were so unknown
I told a dog you were a fine composer.

Why am I afraid or sorry you are dead?
My hands paid contraband to be this still.
My mouth rotted with the truth
To be as tough as wheat before your stone.

Fort Casey, Without Guns

For Rae Tufts

The iron doors we shut on ammo rooms
Slam like a heart attack. Had the guns remained,
Grass would still be busted by July to straw
And riptides groan as current doubles back
In hatred. Concrete walls were hopes
Of pioneers, one shade deeper gray each spring.
From these emplacements, ten-inch cannons tracked
Fifty years of freighters down the strait.
The sea shot out the gunners' eyes with light.
The army moved to Coupeville in defeat.

What's left to save, the riptide will protect.
We joke our way through battlements,
Dim powder huts, the corridors where words explode
And we are skeletons, trapped by a mistake—
The wrong door closed, a turn we didn't make.
We claw at rungs to take us into sky.

Straw bales on the muster ground deny
A need for war. The farmer doesn't care.
The strait can go unguarded, pagan ships
Sail in with slave girls and a threat of fun—
The Stars-And-Stripes torn down—The Constitution
Used to start a fire for the wienie roast.
Only harvest matters. Here, the army
Harvested no enemy. Even boredom cracked—
Contraband steamed down in 'twenty-eight—
The bootleg wink—rum for rotting men.

Best to come here when the picnics peter out.
On dark days, gulls are shells (man will not disarm)

And we can play our war. I am a captain.
Make that cloud salute. The Olympics
Bomb the strait with shadow. In the meadow
Where October green begins, cattle eat
And children point their space guns at us,
Crying boom the booming sea can't hear.

Duwamish Head

That girl upstream was diced by scaling knives—
Scattered in the shack I licked her knees in
Where she tossed me meat and called me dog
And I would dive a dog at her from stars
Wind around my ears—violins and shot.

With salmon gone and industry moved in
Birds don't bite the water. Once this river
Brought a cascade color to the sea.
Now the clouds are cod, crossing on the prowl
Beneath the dredge that heaps a hundred tons
Of crud on barges for the dumping ground.

My vision started at this river mouth,
On a slack tide, trying to catch bullheads
In a hopeless mud. The pier was caving
From the weight of gulls. Wail of tug
And trawl, a town not growing up
Across the bay, rotten pay for kings—
These went by me like the secret dawns
The sea brought in. I saw the seaperch
Turn and briefly flare around a pile
And disappear. I heard bent men
Beg a sole to look less like a stone.

Beyond the squatters and the better homes
Stars were good to dive from. Scattered
In the shack I licked her knees in.
Diced, the paper said, by scaling knives.

2.

River, I have loved, loved badly on your bank.
On your out-tide drain I ride toward the sea
So deep the blue cries out in pain from weight.
Loved badly you and years of misery
In shacks along your bank—cruel women
And their nervous children—fishhooks filed
For easy penetration—cod with cracked necks
Reaching with their gills for one more day.
Last year's birds are scouting for the kill,
Hysterical as always when the smelt run thin.

Jacks don't run. Mills go on polluting
And the river hot with sewage steams.
In bourbon sleep, old men hummed salmon
Home to mountains and the river jammed
With blackmouth, boiled in moonlight while the mills
Boomed honest sparks. October rolled
With dorsal fins and no man ruled the runs.

When I see a stream, I like to say: exactly—
Where else could it run? Trace it back to ice—
Try to find a photo of your cradle—
Rivers jump their beds and don't look back
Regretting they have lost such lovely rides.

I could name those birds, see people
In the clouds. Sight can be polluted
Like a river. When this river asks me:
Where were you when slavs gave up their names
To find good homes on paved streets west of here?

I talk back. What are you, river?
Only water, taking any bed you find.
All you have is current, doubled back

On in-tide, screaming out on out.
I am on your bank, blinded and alive.

3.

Where cod and boys had war, a bolt plant roars.
Sparks are stars. Next sunday, when I die
No drunk will groan my name in spasms
As he vomits last night from the dock.
I have memories of heat upstream.
Her arms and eyes had power like the river
And she imitated salmon with a naked roll.

My vision started at this river mouth
And stuck here (bullhead in the mud)
A third of what could be a lifetime.
The city blares and fishermen are rich.
Tugs and trawls repainted slide to ports
And perch found better color in the sea.

My fins are hands. The river, once
So verbal drifts with such indifference
By me I am forced to shout my name:
Backing up on in-tide, screaming out on out—
River, I have loved, loved badly on your bank.

Scattered in the shack I licked her knees in—
Beyond her, nothing, just the Indian
I use so often infantile in dreams
Of easy winters, five day runs of silvers,
Festive bakes, the passing of the jacks
To sand pools promised by the rain.

To know is to be alien to rivers.
This river helped me play an easy role—

To be alone, to drink, to fail.
The world goes on with money. A tough cat
Dove here from a shingle mill on meat
That glittered as it swam. The mill is gone.
The cat is ground. If I say love
Was here, along the river, show me bones
Of cod, scales and blood, faces in the clouds
So thick they jam the sky with laughter.

Carolyn Kizer was born in Spokane, Washing-ton. She is a graduate of Sarah Lawrence College and a fellow of Columbia University. Her first collection of poems, The Ungrateful Garden, *appeared in 1961. She lives in Seattle, where she edits the quarterly magazine,* Poetry Northwest.

The Great Blue Heron

M.A.K., September, 1880-September, 1955

As I wandered on the beach
I saw the heron standing
Sunk in the tattered wings
He wore as a hunchback's coat.
Shadow without a shadow,
Hung on invisible wires
From the top of a canvas day,
What scissors cut him out?
Superimposed on a poster
Of summer by the strand
Of a long-decayed resort,
Poised in the dusty light
Some fifteen summers ago;
I wondered, an empty child,
"Heron, whose ghost are you?"

I stood on the beach alone,
In the sudden chill of the burned.
My thought raced up the path.
Pursuing it, I ran
To my mother in the house
And led her to the scene.
The spectral bird was gone.
But her quick eye saw him drifting
Over the highest pines
On vast, unmoving wings.
Could they be those ashen things,
So grounded, unwieldy, ragged,
A pair of broken arms
That were not made for flight?
In the middle of my loss

I realized she knew:
My mother knew what he was.

O great blue heron, now
That the summer house has burned
So many rockets ago,
So many smokes and fires
And beach-lights and water-glow
Reflecting pin-wheel and flare:
The old logs hauled away,
The pines and driftwood cleared
From that bare strip of shore
Where dozens of children play;
Now there is only you
Heavy upon my eye.
Why have you followed me here,
Heavy and far away?
You have stood there patiently
For fifteen summers and snows,
Denser than my repose,
Bleaker than any dream,
Waiting upon the day
When, like gray smoke, a vapor
Floating into the sky,
A handful of paper ashes,
My mother would drift away.

By the Riverside

Do not call from memory—
all numbers have changed.
From the cover of the telephone directory

Once I lived at a Riverside
1-3-7-5, by a real stream, Hangman's Creek,
Named from an old pine, down the hill
On which three Indians died. As a child,
I modeled the Crucifixion on that tree
Because I'd heard two Indians were thieves
Strung up by soldiers from Fort Wright in early days,
But no one remembered who the third one was.

Once, in winter, I saw an old Indian wade,
Breaking the thin ice with his thighs.
His squaw crouched modestly in the water,
But he stood up tall, buck-naked. "Cold!" he said,
Proud of his iron flesh, the color of rust,
And his bold manhood, roused by the shock of ice.
He grinned as he spoke, struck his hard chest a blow
Once, with his fist. . . . So I call, from memory,
That tall old Indian, standing in the water.

And I am not put off by an operator
Saying, "Sor-ree, the lion is busy. . . ."
Then, I would tremble, seeing a real lion
Trammeled in endless, golden coils of wire,
Pawing a switchboard in some mysterious
Central office, where animals ran the world,
As I knew they did. To the brave belonged the power.
Christ was a brave, beneath the gauzy clout.

I whispered to the corners of my room, where lions
Crowded at night, blotting the walls with shadows,

As the wind tore at a gutter beneath the eaves,
Moaned with the power of quiet animals
And the old pine, down the hill,
                              where Indians hung:
Telling my prayers, not on a pale-faced Sunday
Nor to a red God, who could walk on water
When winter hardened, and the ice grew stronger.
Now I call up god-head and manhood, both,
As they emerged for a child by the Riverside.
But they are all dead Indians now. They answer
Only to me. The numbers have not changed.

A Widow in Wintertime

Last night a baby gargled in the throes
Of a fatal spasm. My children are all grown
Past infant strangles; so, reassured, I knew
Some other baby perished in the snow.
But no. The cat was making love again.

Later, I went down and let her in.
She hung her tail, flagging from her sins.
Though she'd eaten, I forked out another dinner,
Being myself hungry all ways, and thin
From metaphysic famines she knows nothing of,

The feckless beast! Even so, resemblances
Were on my mind: female and feline, though
She preens herself from satisfaction, and does
Not mind lying even in snow. She is
Lofty and bedraggled, without need to choose.

As an ex-animal, I look fondly on
Her excesses and simplicities, and would not return
To them; taking no marks for what I have become,
Merely that my nine lives peal in my ears again
And again, ring in these austerities,

These arbitrary disciplines of mine,
Most of them trivial: like covering
The children on my way to bed, and trying
To live well enough alone, and not to dream
Of grappling in the snow, claws plunged in fur,

Or waken in a caterwaul of dying.

Tying One on in Vienna

Variations on a theme of H.H.

I have been, faithfully, to the 39 birthplaces of Beethoven;
To 39 birthplaces of Beethoven have I been.
Reborn, every time, to the wrath of landladies
Who objected to the noise,
He had to move on.
Damn and bless your peripetia, Beethoven.
I am above your Meer und Sturme, I have won my haven
On high, below, in a cozy rathskeller in Vienna.

I tip the whole world down my throat,
Thirsty as Beethoven.
If I were home, I'd float on an ice cube like a polar bear
In my terrible fur, bulky as Beethoven,
Dipping my toes in an ocean of whiskey.
But here is a whole world in a golden brew:
Viennese cathedrals, where Mongol troops, I'm told,
Took pot-shots at gargoyles, to destroy their evil-eyes—
Never mind: gargoyles will rise again, gargle golden wine,
Giggle in rathskellers; Luther broke things too,
Or his followers did. Give me a golden Pope
Who wallows in artifacts, tithes a thousand villages
For one gold goblet: O I see all the Leos of all the Romes
In this glass: Agamemnon's cup, the brilliant vessels
Of Vaphio, with ruminating bulls, bulls grazing,
And bulls chased round and round the bowl by crazy
    Schliemann.
Turks and Hellenes, Mongols, Shakespearean scholars—
    Hegel!
Continuity is all!
Changing the petticoat guard at the palace of Paul
And Frederika; orange groves, All Souls' Day, 4th of Juiy

parades;
Vienna, Spokane, Los Angeles County—even Hamburg. . . .
And over all others, the face of my lover,
A man with the brain of an angel!

Beloved, thou art fair,
With hair the color of Solomon's beard
And a big head, like Beethoven.
David the Goliath, patron saint of Florence,
Has a navel like a pigeon's swimming-pool;
You are the David of the Galleria dell'Accademia
Whose navel is a little golden bowl
In which I plunge my nose—Oh, what a heavenly odor!
Landlord, hold me up by the hair
Before I drown!

Der brave Mann! We sit here together
Drinking like brother and sister,
We hug each other like sister and brother
And he speaks to me of the power of love.
I drink to the health of my ex-husband
And other enemies, known and unknown.
I FORGIVE ALL LOUSY POETS
AS THEY SHALL FORGIVE ME.
I weep in an excess of feeling!

Then I cry to him, "Landlord, where are the twelve apostles,
The holy hogsheads, hidden in the back room
Where they preach to the United Nations?
Lead me to them, in their plain wooden jackets,
Looking like Mennonite farmers. Their souls are more
    radiant
Than the Court of St. James's, than the Fabergé eggs
In the Hermitage Museum. . . .
Purple and Gold! My old High School colors!"

O those grand autumn days, when we crushed Immaculate
    Conception,
And the Society of Jesus provided cheerleaders,
Though both teams flopped down on the field to pray
Just before game-time. And I debated the girls from the
    convent
On, "Resolved: We should have government ownership of
    railroads"
And God was on my side, the affirmative.
Though I spoke with the tongue of gargoyle and angel,
God and I lost, because the girls of St. Mary's
Kept their skirts over their knees and their hands folded,
While I waved my wild hair, and bit my nails
In an excess of feeling. . . .

Hooray! I'm being fanned by palm trees!
And the scent of orange groves in the sweet San Fernando
    Valley
North of Los Angeles, where I spent my childhood;
What an odor of myrrh is rising from a thousand navels!
Reel on, you rivers of the world!
Even the rathskeller door, with its broken hinges
Since the Russian troops hammered it down, looking for
    girls,
Even the old door, wounded with bayonet marks,
Dances and reels, and my soul staggers for joy,
And we are all healed together, noble Viennese landlord!

He will steer me upstairs to the daylight,
Du braver Ratskellermeister,
And we'll see, though the gargoyles are broken,
There are angels on the roofs of the cathedral,
On all the roofs—see those angels sitting there like
    pigeons?
Angels of Heine and Rilke, all drunk. Singing,

Hallelujah and Yippee! If there were a sun overhead
It would be red like the nose of a drunkard,
Behind all that Viennese rain, as drunk as Beethoven
Every time he was born. The soul of the world is a nose,
A nose in a navel. The red sun sets in the navel of heaven.
God save a disorderly world, and the wild United Nations!
The twelve holy hogsheads will roll forth on their keg legs
And save us all: poets, Mongolians, landlords & ladies, mad
    musicians.
And we'll reel on together, sing in a widening circle,
Hooray for purple and gold, for liquor and angels!

Winter Song

on a line from Arthur Waley

So I go on, tediously on and on . . .
We are separated, finally, not by death but life:
We can cling to the dead, but the living break away.

On my birthday the waxwings arrive in the garden,
Strip the trees bare as my barren heart.
I put out suet and bread for December birds:
Hung from evergreen branches, greasy grey
Ornaments for the rites of winter solstice.

How can you and I meet face to face
After our triumphant love?
After our failure?

Since this isolation, it is always cold.
My clothes don't fit. My hair refuses to obey.
And, for the first time, I permit
These little anarchies of flesh and object.
Together, they flick me towards some final defeat.

Thinking of you, I am suddenly old . . .
A mute spectator as the months roll by.
I have tried to put you out of my mind forever.

Home isn't here. It went away with you,
Disappearing in the space of a breath,
In the time one takes to open a foreknown letter.
If I flung myself on the ground it would bruise like stone.
There are clouds between me and the watery light.

Truly, I try to flourish, to find pleasure
Without an endless reference to you
Who made the years and days seem worth enduring.

Night Sounds

imitated from the Chinese

The moonlight on my bed keeps me awake;
Living alone now, aware of the voices of evening,
A child weeping at nightmares, the faint love-cries of a
    woman,
Everything tinged by terror or nostalgia.

No heavy, impassive back to nudge with one foot
While coaxing, "Wake up and hold me,"
When the moon's creamy beauty is transformed
Into a map of impersonal desolation.

But, restless in this mock dawn of moonlight
That so chills the spirit, I alter our history:
You were never able to lie quite peacefully at my side,
Not the night through. Always withholding something.

Awake before morning, restless and uneasy,
Trying not to disturb me, you would leave my bed
While I lay there rigidly, feigning sleep.
Still—the night was nearly over, the light not as cold
As a full cup of moonlight.

And there were the lovely times when, to the skies' cold *No*
You cried to me, *Yes!* Impaled me with affirmation.
Now when I call out in fear, not in love, there is no answer.
Nothing speaks in the dark but the distant voices,
A child with the moon on his face, a dog's hollow cadence.

Summer Near the River

from *The Book of Songs*

I have carried my pillow to the windowsill
And try to sleep, with my damp arms crossed upon it
But no breeze stirs the tepid morning.
Only I stir. . . . Come, tease me a little!
With such cold passion, so little teasing play,
How long can we endure our life together?

No use. I put on your long dressing-gown;
The untied sash trails over the dusty floor.
I kneel by the window, prop up your shaving mirror
And pluck my eyebrows.
I don't care if the robe slides open
Revealing a crescent of belly, a tan thigh.
I can accuse that non-existent breeze. . . .

I am as monogamous as the North Star
But I don't want you to know it. You'd only take advantage.
While you are as fickle as spring sunlight.
All right, sleep! The cat means more to you than I.
I can rouse you, but then you swagger out.
I glimpse you from the window, striding towards the river.

When you return, reeking of fish and beer,
There is salt dew in your hair. Where have you been?
Your clothes weren't that wrinkled hours ago, when you left.
You couldn't have loved someone else, after loving me!
I sulk and sigh, dawdling by the window.
Later, when you hold me in your arms,
It seems, for a moment, the river ceases flowing.

Amusing Our Daughters

For Robert Creeley

after Po Chu-I

We don't lack people here on the Northern coast,
But they are people one meets, not people one cares for.
So I bundle my daughters into the car
And with my brother poets, go to visit you, brother.

Here come your guests! A swarm of strangers and children;
But the strangers write verses, the children are daughters
    like yours.
We bed down on mattresses, cots, roll up on the floor:
Outside, burly old fruit trees in mist and rain;
In every room, bundles asleep like larvae.

We waken and count our daughters. Otherwise, nothing
    happens.
You feed them sweet rolls and melon, drive them all to the
    zoo;
Patiently, patiently, ever the father, you answer their
    questions.
Later we eat again, drink, listen to poems.
Nothing occurs, though we are aware you have three
    daughters
Who last year had four. But even death becomes part of our
    ease:
Poems, parenthood, sorrow, all we have learned
From these, of tenderness, holds us together
In the center of life, entertaining daughters
By firelight, with cake and songs.

You, my brother, are a good and violent drinker,
Good at reciting short-line or long-line poems.
In time we will lose all our daughters, you and I,
Be temperate, venerable, content to stay in one place,
Sending our messages over the mountains and waters.

The Skein

from the Chinese

Moonlight through my gauze curtains
Turns them to nets for snaring wild birds,
Turns them into woven traps, into shrouds.
The old, restless grief keeps me awake.
I wander around, holding a scarf or shawl,
In the muffled moonlight I wander around
Folding it carefully, shaking it out again.
Everyone says my old love is happy.
I wish they said he was coming back to me.
I hesitate here, my scarf like a skein of yarn
Binding my two hands loosely
   that would reach for paper and pen.
So I memorize these lines,
Dew on the scarf dappling my nightdress also.
O love long gone, it is raining in our room!
So I memorize these lines
   without salutation, without close.

From *Pro Femina*

I will speak about women of letters, for I'm in the racket.
Our biggest successes to date? Old maids to a woman.
And our saddest conspicuous failures? The married
    spinsters
On loan to the husbands they treat like surrogate fathers.
Thing of that crew of self-pitiers, not-very-distant,
Who carried the torch for themselves and got first-degree
    burns.
Or the sad sonneteers, toast-and-teasdales we loved at
    thirteen;
Middle-aged virgins seducing the puerile anthologists
Through lust-of-the-mind, barbiturate-drenched Camilles
With continuous periods, murmuring softly on sofas,
When poetry wasn't a craft but a sickly effluvium,
The air thick with incense, musk, and emotional blackmail.
I suppose they reacted from an earlier womanly modesty
When too many girls were scabs to their stricken sisterhood,
Impugning our sex to stay in good with the men,
Commencing their insecure bluster. How they must have
    swaggered
When women themselves indorsed their own inferiority!
Vestals, vassals and vessels, rolled into several,
They took notes in rolling syllabics, in careful journals,
Aiming to please a posterity that despises them.
But we'll always have traitors who swear that a woman
    surrenders
Her Supreme Function, by equating Art with aggression
And failure with Femininity. Still, it's just as unfair
To equate Art with Femininity, like a prettily-packaged
    commodity
When we are custodians of the world's best-kept secret:
Merely the private lives of one-half of humanity.

But even with masculine dominance, we mares and
      mistresses
Produced some sleek saboteuses, making their cracks
Which the porridge-brained males of the day were too thick
      to perceive,
Mistaking young hornets for perfectly harmless
      bumblebees.
Being thought innocuous rouses some women to frenzy;
They try to be ugly by aping the ways of the men
And succeed. Swearing, sucking cigars and scorching the
      bedspread,
Slopping straight shots, eyes blotted, vanity-blown
In the expectation of praise: *she writes like a man!*
This drives other women mad in a mist of chiffon
(one poetess draped her gauze over red flannels, a practical
      feminist).

But we're emerging from all that, more or less,
Except for some ladylike laggards, and Quarterly priestesses
Who flog men for fun, and kick women to maim
      competition.
Now, if we struggle abnormally, we may almost seem
      normal;
If we submerge our self-pity in disciplined industry;
If we stand up and be hated, and swear not to sleep with
      editors;
If we regard ourselves formally, respecting our true
      limitations
Without making an unseemly show of trying to unfreeze
      our assets;
Keeping our heads and our pride while remaining unmarried;
And if wedded, kill guilt in its tracks when we stack up the
      dishes
And defect to the typewriter. And if mothers, believe in the
      luck of our children,

68

Whom we forbid to devour us, whom we shall not devour,
And the luck of our husbands and lovers, who keep free
    women.

William Stafford was born in Hutchinson, Kansas, in 1914. He was educated at the University of Kansas and the State University of Iowa. He has published two collections of Poetry, West of Your City (1960) and Traveling Through the Dark (1962). He teaches English Literature and Composition at Lewis and Clark College in Portland, Oregon.

Found in a Storm

A storm that needed a mountain
met it where we were:
we woke up in a gale
that was reasoning with our tent,
and all the persuaded snow
streaked along, guessing the ground.

We turned from that curtain, down.
But sometime we will turn
back to the curtain and go
by plan through an unplanned storm,
disappearing into the cold,
meanings in search of a world.

Bulletin

At five o'clock one morning according to the chart
the submarine Hysteria surfaced in the dark.
The cutter Aurora glimpsed it sharking toward the reef.

In all the coral ocean there is no pattern more tropic,
more shadowed, more fleeting, than this configuration,
a slanting destiny that might have been.

We count those travelers lucky who snug in the bunk
    wake up
to feel the intimate tremble, the far-off spiral tooting,
and the steady tearing silk of that rare sea.

Believing What I Know

A lake on the map of Canada
may forget in the snow—
in the spring be gone.

Imagine flower-eyes
nodding a little breeze,
looking at the land where the lake was.

Many things that were true
disappeared, grew up in grass,
and now hide from flowers that stare.

I learn from the land. Some day
like a field I may take the next thing
so well that whatever is will be me.

Traveling Through the Dark

Traveling through the dark I found a deer
dead on the edge of the Wilson River road.
It is usually best to roll them into the canyon:
that road is narrow; to swerve might make more dead.

By glow of the tail-light I stumbled back of the car
and stood by the heap, a doe, a recent killing;
she had stiffened already, almost cold.
I dragged her off; she was large in the belly.

My fingers touching her side brought me the reason—
her side was warm; her fawn lay there waiting,
alive, still, never to be born.
Beside that mountain road I hesitated.

The car aimed ahead its lowered parking lights;
under the hood purred the steady engine.
I stood in the glare of the warm exhaust turning red;
around our group I could hear the wilderness listen.

I thought hard for us all—my only swerving—,
then pushed her over the edge into the river.

To a Colleague Fulbrighting in Finland

Our near course ends with you gone far
past ice through waves to land
more level than the sea and forested
till it forgets to stop, a fringe
that keeps on weaving laced by streams and wolves.

My fingers drum this desk, and horses
bring the foreign sleigh from night
into my eyes that, waiting, pierce the roof
into the dark, but short of any object
or wide of how to find any center for the sky.

"We live our story, stories as our guide;
our heroes loom because we need them;
a drama is a local model of something
that pervades everything; even the act
of denying a book is part of its meaning,"

You said. "Literature frees in a special way
the real life that is oppressed by living."
Now I am puzzled more than other people.
Often I hear owls imitating the Indians;
alone I face the depth of surfaces.

At a ditch I pass every day an animal dives.
I try to catch it but like it to get away.
I hope, with all my failures, never to really fail,
and if the clock brings me to any new road
never to take it, so long as this road goes—

Our road that bends hillsides at need
and follows a story lived out by its walkers.

Because you taught so well and went so far,
all else is near. So scholars learn the world,
you said. "We live so far the wind is ours."

In the Museum

Like that, I put the next thing in your hand—
this piece of rock the farthest climbers found,
or this, a broken urn volcano-finished.

Later you'll walk out and say, "Where's home?"
There will be something lacking in each room,
a part you held and casually laid down.

You never can get back, but there'll be other
talismans. You have learned to falter
in this good way: stand still, walk on, remember—

Let one by one things come alive like fish
and swim away into their future waves.

A Dedication

We stood by the library. It was an August night.
Priests and sisters of hundreds of unsaid creeds
passed us going their separate pondered roads.
We watched them cross under the corner light.

Freights on the edge of town were carrying away
flatcars of steel to be made into secret guns;
we knew, being human, that they were enemy guns,
and we were somehow vowed to poverty.

No one stopped or looked long or held out a hand.
They were following orders received from hour to hour,
so many signals, all strange, from a foreign power:
But tomorrow, you whispered, *peace may flow over the land*.

At that corner in a flash of lightning we two stood;
that glimpse we had will stare through the dark forever:
on the poorest roads we would be walkers and beggars,
toward some deathless meeting involving a crust of bread.

Walking West

Anyone with quiet pace who
walks a gray road in the West
may hear a badger underground where
in deep flint another time is

Caught by flint and held forever,
the quiet pace of God stopped still.
Anyone who listens walks on
time that dogs him single file,

To mountains that are far from people,
the face of the land gone gray like flint.
Badgers dig their little lives there,
quiet-paced the land lies gaunt,

The railroad dies by a yellow depot,
town falls away toward a muddy creek.
Badger-gray the sod goes under
a river of wind, a hawk on a stick.

Ultimate Problems

In the Aztec design God crowds
into the little pea that is rolling
out of the picture.
All the rest extends bleaker
because God has gone away.

In the White Man design, though,
no pea is there.
God is everywhere,
but hard to see.
The Aztecs frown at this.

How do you know He is everywhere?
And how did He get out of the pea?

Late at Night

Falling separate into the dark
the hailstone yelps of geese pattered
through our roof; startled we listened.

Those V's of direction swept by unseen
so orderly that we paused. But then
faltering back through their circle they came.

Were they lost up there in the night?
They always knew the way, we thought.
You looked at me across the room:—

We live in a terrible season.

On an Island in the San Juans

Rabbits here have chosen their holes
different ways—the more neurotic
the rabbit the deeper the hole; all
happily squat at their various right levels
playing nibble-nose and wondering why
everyone doesn't adjust by footwork,
or just flatten its versatile ears.

Birds here do not care to contest our
way of owning an island. Their
way adjusts up or down so easily—
turn here, there, perch or glide,
and song through any thicket—
that our irrelevant contracts never
even trill their high ownership.

But could we turn by any tide
always back to here, even then
the slant of the cove would steepen,
darken, refuse the light like a fir:—
we are oriented for other use.
We wave gamely along the rail to a friend
as wild as ourselves—a man or a woman:

"See you (or someone) here (or somewhere)
like this (waving goodby) next year."

Peace Walk

We wondered what our walk should mean,
taking that un-march quietly;
the sun stared at our signs—"Thou shalt not kill."

Men by a tavern said, "Those foreigners..."
to a woman with a fur, who turned away—
like an elevator going down, their look at us.

Along a curb, their signs lined across,
a picket line stopped and stared
the whole width of the street, at ours: "Unfair."

Above our heads the sound truck blared—
by the park, under the autumn trees—
it said that love could fill the atmosphere:

Occur, slow the other fallout, unseen,
on islands everywhere—fallout falling
unheard. We held our poster up to shade our eyes.

At the end we just walked away;
no one was there to tell us where to leave the signs.

An Address to the Vacationers
at Cape Lookout

The whole weight of the ocean smashes on rock;
the sun hounds the night; gulls ravel the edge.
Here it is better to allow for what happens, all of it—
the part assumed, the lie that keeps a rendezvous
with proof, the wickerwork that disguises the iron:
this place is too real for that blame
people pin on each other, for honor or dishonor.
>   Have you noticed how uninvited
>   anything pure is? Be brave—there is such a thing
>   as helping history get on with its dirty work.

When the home folk tell you goodby
they shouldn't *bid* you goodby, that corrupted, wise way,
nor burden you with too great a gift; and I
wouldn't burden you, except with one great gift:
the cold, the world that spins in cold space—
to be able to walk away, not writhe in regret
or twist in the torture bush. After all,
there is such a thing as justice in friendship.
>   All of the time, we know how uninvited
>   anything pure is: here something big lifts us
>   outside, scorns our bravery or fear.

What disregards people does people good.

Watching the Jet Planes Dive

We must go back and find a trail on the ground
back of the forest and mountain on the slow land;
we must begin to circle on the intricate sod.
By such wild beginnings without help we may find
the small trail on through the buffalo-bean vines.

We must go back with noses and the palms of our hands,
and climb over the map in far places, everywhere,
and lie down whenever there is doubt and sleep there.
If roads are unconnected we must make a path,
no matter how far it is, or how lowly we arrive.

We must find something forgotten by everyone alive,
and make some fabulous gesture when the sun goes down
as they do by custom in little Mexico towns
where they crawl for some ritual up a rocky steep.
The jet planes dive; we must travel on our knees.

Letter from Oregon

Mother, here there are shadowy salmon;
ever their sides argue up the falls.
Watching them plunge with fluttering gills,
I thought back through Wyoming where I came from.

The gleaming sides of my train glimmered
up over passes and arrowed through shoals
of aspen fluttering in a wind of yellow.
Only the sky stayed true; I turned,

Justifying space through those miles of Wyoming
till the wave of the land was quelled by the stars;
then tunnels of shadow led me far
through doubt, and I was home.

Mother, even home was doubtful;
many slip into the sea and are gone for years,
just as I boarded the six-fifteen there.
Over the bar I have leaped outward.

Somewhere in the ocean beyond Laramie
when that grass folded low in the dark
a lot fin waved, and I felt the beat
of the old neighborhood stop, on our street.

Lore

Dogs that eat fish edging tidewater die—
Some kind of germ, or too much vitamin.
Indian dogs ate copper for a cure;
a penny will save a spaniel that ate salmon.

On the shore beachcombers find a float
of glass the Japanese used on a net
that broke away deep over the side of the world
and slid blue on the beach here as a gift.

Pieces of driftwood turn into time
and wedge among rocks the breakers pound.
Finding such wrought-work you wonder if the tide
brings in something else when the sun goes down.

Outside

The least little sound sets the coyotes walking,
walking the edge of our comfortable earth.
We look inward, but all of them
are looking toward us as they walk the earth.

We need to let animals loose in our houses,
the wolf to escape with a pan in his teeth,
and streams of animals toward the horizon
racing with something silent in each mouth.

For all we have taken into our keeping
and polished with our hands belongs to a truth
greater than ours, in the animals' keeping.
Coyotes are circling around our truth.

At the Bomb Testing Site

At noon in the desert a panting lizard
waited for history, its elbows tense,
watching the curve of a particular road
as if something might happen.

It was looking at something farther off
than people could see, an important scene
acted in stone for little selves
at the flute end of consequences.

There was just a continent without much on it
under a sky that never cared less.
Ready for a change, the elbows waited.
The hands gripped hard on the desert.

Fall Wind

Pods of summer crowd around the door;
I take them in the autumn of my hands.

Last night I heard the first cold wind outside;
the wind blew soft, and yet I shiver twice:

Once for thin walls, once for the sound of time.

In the Night Desert

The Apache word for love twists
    then numbs the tongue:
Uttered once clear, said—
    never that word again.

"Cousin," you call, or "Sister" and one
    more word that spins
In the dust: a talk-flake
    chipped like obsidian.

The girl who hears this flake and
    follows you into the dark
Turns at a touch: the night desert
    forever behind her back.

David Wagoner was born in Massillon, Ohio, in 1926. He was educated at Pennsylvania State College and Indiana University. He has published three novels, The Man in the Middle, Money Money Money, *and* Rock. *In 1965 his fourth novel,* Nightlatch, *will be published. His third collection of poems,* The Nesting Ground, *appeared in 1963. His earlier poetry collections were* Dry Sun, Dry Wind *and* A Place to Stand. *He is at present an Associate Professor of English at the University of Washington.*

After Consulting My Yellow Pages

All went well today in the barbers' college:
The razor handles pointed gracefully outward,
The clippers were singing like locusts. And far away
On the fox farms, the red and silver sun brushed lightly
Tail after tail. Happily, the surveyors
Measured the downhill pasture through a theodolite,
Untroubled by birchtrees. The makers of fraternal regalia
Conceived a new star-burst, and the parakeet
In the green bird hospital was coaxed out of danger.
Business came flying out of the horse-meat market,
And under the skillful world, the conduits groped
Forward, heavy with wires, to branch at the lake.
Fish brokers prodded salmon on the walloping dock.
The manifold continuous forms and the luminous products
Emerged, endlessly shining, while the cooling towers
Poured water over themselves like elephants.
Busily the deft hands of the locksmith and wig-maker
In basement and loft, in the magnifying light,
Turned at their labors. The universal joints,
Hose-couplings, elastic hosiery, shingles and shakes,
The well-beloved escrow companies, the heat-exchangers,
Bead-stringers, makers of disappearing beds,
The air-compressors randy with oxygen—
All sprang, remarkably, out of the swinging doors.

And where were you? What did you do today?

Diary

At Monday dawn, I climbed into my skin
And went to see the money. There were the shills:
I conned them—oh, the coins fell out of their mouths,
And paint peeled from the walls like dollar bills.
Below their money-belts, I did them in.

All day Tuesday, grand in my underwear,
I shopped for the world, bought basements and airplanes,
Bargained for corners and pedestrians
And, when I'd marketed the elms away,
Swiped from the water, stole down to the stones.

Suddenly Wednesday offered me my shirt,
Trousers, and shoes. I put them on to dream
Of the one-way stairway and the skittering cloud,
Of the dangerous, footsore crossing at the heart
Where trees, rivers, and stones reach for the dead.

And the next day meant the encircling overcoat
Wherein I sweltered, woolly as a ram:
From butt to swivel, I hoofed it on the loam,
Exacting tribute from the flock in the grass.
My look passed through the werewolf to the lamb.

Friday shied backwards, pulling off my clothes:
The overcoat fell open like a throat;
Shirt-tail and shoe went spidery as a thought,
And covetous drawers whipped knee-deep in a knot.
My skin in a spiral tapered into gold.

And it was naked Saturday for love
Again: the graft grew milky at a kiss.

I lay on the week with money, lust, and vapor,
Megalomania, fear, the tearing-off,
And love in a coil. On Sunday, I wrote this.

Observations from the Outer Edge

I pass the abrupt end of the woods, and stop.
I'm standing on a cliff as sheer as a step
Where the ground, like the ground floor of a nightmare,
Has slipped a notch six hundred rocky feet
And left itself in the lurch. My shoes go dead.
Not looking yet, I let my heart sneak back,

But feel like the fall-guy ending a Western,
The heavy, bound to topple from the edge
And disappear with terrible gravity.
I put my hand out in the separate air
With nothing under it, but it feels nothing.
This is no place for putting my foot down,

So I shout my name, but can't scare up an echo.
No one inside this canyon wants to be me.
I manage to look down. Not much to envy:
The silent, immobile rapids, the toy pines,
A fisherman stuck in the shallows like an agate—
A world so far away, it can quit moving

And I wouldn't know the difference. I've seen it before
At the ends of hallways, the far sides of windows,
Shrinking from sight. Down is no worse than across.
Whether it's sky, horizon, or ground zero,
A piece of space will take whatever comes
From any direction—climbing, walking, or falling.

I remember a newsreel—a man holding a baby
Over the Grand Canyon on a stick:
The kid hung on and grinned for the camera.
I grab the nearest branch just to make sure

It isn't death down there, looking like hell.
Even a mountain goat will go to pieces

Standing on glass suspended in the air,
But men created with a jerkier balance
Can learn to fix their eyes on a safe place.
Trembling somewhere,
The acrophobiac Primum Mobile
Clings to his starry axle, staring sideways.

Elegy for Simon Corl, Botanist

With wildflowers bedded in his mind,
My blind great-uncle wrote a book.
His lips and beard were berry-stained,
Wrist broken like a shepherd's crook.

His door leaned open to the flies,
And May, like tendrils, wandered in.
The earth rose gently to his knees;
The clouds moved closer than his skin.

Sun against ear, he heard the slight
Stamen and pistil touch for days,
Felt pollen cast aslant like light
Into the shadows of his eyes.

When autumn stalked the leaves, he curled;
His fingers ripened like the sky;
His ink ran to a single word,
And the straight margin went awry.

When frost lay bristling on the weeds,
He smoothed it with a yellow thumb,
Followed his white cane to the woods
Between the saxifrage and thyme,

And heard the hornets crack like ice,
Felt worms arch backward in the snow;
And while the mites died under moss,
The clean scar sang across his brow.

Murder Mystery

After the murder, like parades of Fools
The bungling supernumeraries come,
Sniffing at footprints, looking under rugs,
Clasping the dead man with prehensile tools.
Lens against nose, false beard down to his knees,
The Hawkshaw enters, hoists his bag of tricks,
And passes out suspicion like lemonade:
"Where were you when the victim—" "In my room."
"Didn't you ask him whether—" "Double locks."
"Who switched the glasses on the—" "Crippled legs."
"Why were the ballroom curtains—" "Mad for years."
Then, tripping on clues, they wander through the house,
And search each other, frighten themselves with guns,
Ransack the kitchen and the sherry bins,
And dance in the bushes with the cats and dogs.

"Where is he?" says the Captain. "Nobody cares."
"We did it!" scream the butler and the maid.
"I did it too!" the jolly doctor cries.
And all join in—detective, counterfoil,
Ingenue, hero, and the family ghosts—
And, flapping like tongues, the trapdoors babble guilt,
The window-boxes, closets understairs,
Whatnots and chandeliers, grandfather clocks,
The sealed-up attic with its litter of bones—
All of them shake, and pour their secrets out.
And the happy party, bearing aloft the dead,
Handcuffed and drunk, go singing towards the jail;
Stage-hands roll up their sleeves, fold up the lawn,
Dismantle the hedges and the flowerbed,
Then follow, hauling the mansion, to confess.

Meanwhile, in another place—their figures cold,
Both turned to shadows by a single pain,
Bloodless together—the killer and the slain
Have kissed each other in the wilderness,
Touching soft hands and staring at the world.

The Fruit of the Tree

With a wall and a ditch between us, I watched the gate-
    legged dromedary
Creak open from her sleep and come head-first toward me
As I held out three rust-mottled, tough pears, the color of
    camels.
When I tossed one, she made no move to catch it; whatever
    they eat
Lies still and can wait: the roots and sticks, the scrag-ends of
    brambles.

She straddled, dipping her neck; grey lips and lavender
    tongue,
Which can choose the best of thorns, thrust the pear to her
    gullet.
Choking, she mouthed it; her ruminating jaw swung up;
Her eyes lashed out. With a groan she crushed it down,
And ecstasy swept her down into the ditch, till her chin

And her pointed, prolonged face sat on the wall. She stared
At me, inventor and founder of pears. I emptied my sack.
She ate them painfully, clumsy with joy, her withers
    trembling,
Careless of dust on the bitten and dropped halves, ignoring
    flies,
Making her own music, needing no waiters or awnings.

When she gazed at me again, our mouths were both deserted.
I walked away with myself. She watched me disappear,
Then with a rippling trudge went back to her stable
To snort, to browse on hay, to remember my sack forever.
She'd been used to having no pears, but hadn't known it.

Imagine the hostile runners, the biters of burnouses,
Coughers and spitters, whose legs can kick at amazing
    angles—
Their single humps would carry us willingly over dunes
Through sandstorms and the swirling djinns to the edges of
    oases
If they, from their waterless, intractable hearts, might
    stretch for pears.

The Night of the Sad Women

They are undressing slowly by closed doors,
Unable to find themselves, fading in mirrors
And feeling faint, finding their eyes in time
But seeing, instead, the rooms behind their shoulders

Where nothing is going to work, where photographs
Stand still in frames, arresting other days
When things were turning out. Now turning in,
They are lowering shades and turning off the lights,

But find their fingers lighter than pale linen
At the sinking bedside, seeing their own hands
In front of their faces, wavering like gauze,
Then edging away to search in fallen purses.

But they lose touch. In the middle of their rooms
The night begins, the night of the loose threads
Which hang like spiders' life-lines out of seams
To be ravelled to the floor, but not to end.

After Falling

Sleep lightly, sleep eventfully
That from the jangling backs of your eyes may come the
   harness
Without horses, the trappings of darkness
And a country in pieces wedged across pale hills
And out of the mind—through fields ragged with light
Where the wrong birds out of season
Crouch in the grass, their wings trembling like eyelids.

Sleep watchfully, now, leaning across
The long strands holding the night like reins through clouds
And darkening with them, flourishing into water
Where the rough road divides repeatedly,
Dissolving slowly, streaming into the ground
But springing again, as the birds will,
To climb through wilder country before falling.

The Poets Agree to be Quiet by the Swamp

They hold their hands over their mouths
And stare at the stretch of water.
What can be said has been said before:
Strokes of light like herons' legs in the cattails,
Mud underneath, frogs lying even deeper.
Therefore, the poets may keep quiet.
But the corners of their mouths grin past their hands.
They stick their elbows out into the evening,
Stoop, and begin the ancient croaking.

Leaving Something Behind

A fox at your neck and snakeskin on your feet,
You have gone to the city behind an ivory brooch,
Wearing your charms for and against desire, bearing your
    beauty
Past all the gaping doorways, amazing women on edge
And leading men's eyes astray while skirting mayhem,
And I, for a day, must wish you safe in your skin.

The diggers named her the Minnesota Girl. She was fifteen,
Eight thousand years ago, when she drowned in a glacial
    lake,
Curling to sleep like her sea-snail amulet, holding a turtle-
    shell,
A wolf's tooth, the tine of an antler, carrying somehow
A dozen bones from the feet of water birds. She believed in
    her charms,
But something found her and kept her. She became what she
    wore.

She loved her bones and her own husk of creatures
But left them piecemeal on the branching shore.
Without you, fox paws, elephant haunches, all rattling tails,
Snail's feet, turtles' remote hearts, muzzles of wolves,
Stags' ears, and the tongues of water birds are only them-
    selves.
Come safely back. There was nothing in her arms.

The Man of the House

My father, looking for trouble, would find it
On his hands and knees by hammering on walls
Between the joists or drilling through baseboards
Or crawling into the attic where insulation
Lay under the leaks like sleeping-bags.

It would be something simple as a rule
To be ingenious for, in overalls;
And he would kneel beside it, pouring sweat
Down his red cheeks, glad of a useful day
With something wrong unknown to the landlord.

At those odd times when everything seemed to work
All right, suspiciously all right like silence
In concrete shelters, he'd test whatever hung
Over our heads: such afternoons meant ladders,
Nails in the mouth, flashing and shaking roofs.

In safety shoes going down basement stairs,
He'd flick his rewired rearrangement of lights
And chase all shadows into the coalbin
Where they could watch him, blinking at his glare.
If shadows hadn't worked, he would have made them.

With hands turning to horn against the stone
He'd think on all fours, hunch as if to drink
If his cold chisel broke the cold foundation
And brought dark water pulsing out of clay.
Wrenching at rows of pipes like his cage-bars,

He made them creak in sockets and give way,
But rammed them back, putting his house in order.

Moonlight or rain, after the evening paper,
His mouth lay open under the perfect plaster
To catch the first sweet drop, but none came down.

Out for a Night

It was No, no, no, practicing at a chair,
And No at the wall, and one for the fireplace,
And down the stairs it was No over the railing,
And two for the dirt, and three Noes for the air,

And four in a row rapidly over the bar,
Becoming Maybe, Maybe, from spittoon to mirror,
It was shrugging cheeks on one face after another,
And Perhaps and So-So at both ends of a cigar,

Five, and it was Yes as a matter of fact
Who said it wasn't all the way down the bottle,
It was Hell Yes over and lightly underfoot,
And tongue like a welcome mat for the bartender,

And Yes in the teeth, Yes like a cracked whistle,
And one for you, and two for the rest of us,
Indeed, Indeed, the chair got up on the table,
And Yes got up on the chair and kissed the light

And the light burned, and Yes fell out of the chair,
And the chair slid off the table, and it was Maybe
All over the floor, tilted, it was squat,
And plunge to the rear, and smack lips like a baby,

It was five for the fingers Absolutely,
Four in the corners, it was three for the show,
And two descending eyebrows to make a ceiling,
And No to the knees and chin, and one Goodbye.

A Guide to Dungeness Spit

Out of wild roses down from the switching road between
    pools
We step to an arm of land washed from the sea.
On the windward shore
The combers come from the strait, from narrows and shoals
Far below sight. To leeward, floating on trees
In a blue cove, the cormorants
Stretch to a point above us, their wings held out like skysails.
Where shall we walk? First, put your prints to the sea,
Fill them, and pause there:
Seven miles to the lighthouse, curved yellow-and-grey miles
Tossed among kelp, abandoned with bleaching rooftrees,
Past reaches and currents;
And we must go afoot at a time when the tide is heeling.
Those whistling overhead are Canada geese;
Some on the waves are loons,
And more on the sand are pipers. There, Bonaparte's gulls
Settle a single perch. Those are sponges.
Those are the ends of bones.
If we cross to the inner shore, the grebes and goldeneyes
Rear themselves and plunge through the still surface,
Fishing below the dunes
And rising alarmed, higher than waves. Those are cockle-
    shells.
And these are the dead. I said we would come to these.
Stoop to the stones.
Overturn one: the grey-and-white, inch-long crabs come
    pulsing
And clambering from their hollows, tiptoeing sideways.
They lift their pincers
To defend the dark. Let us step this way. Follow me closely
Past snowy plovers bustling among sand fleas.

114

The air grows dense.
You must decide now whether we shall walk for miles and
    miles
And whether all birds are the young of other creatures
Or their own young ones,
Or simply their old selves because they die. One falls,
And the others touch him webfoot or with claws,
Treading him for the ocean.
This is called sanctuary. Those are feathers and scales.
We both go into mist, and it hooks behind us.
Those are foghorns.
Wait, and the bird on the high root is a snowy owl
Facing the sea. Its flashing yellow eyes
Turn past us and return;
And turning from the calm shore to the breakers, utterly
    still,
They lead us by the bay and through the shallows,
Buoy us into the wind.
Those are tears. Those are called houses, and those are
    people.
Here is a stairway past the whites of our eyes.
All our distance
Has ended in the light. We climb to the light in spirals,
And look, between us we have come all the way,
And it never ends
In the ocean, the spit and image of our guided travels.
Those are called ships. We are called lovers.
There lie the mountains.